RENEW YOUR MIND

By Vivian Daniels

Published by Vivian Daniels
© Vivian Daniels 2018

The rights of Vivian Daniels to be identified as the author of this work have been asserted by her in accordance with the Copyright, Designs and Patents Act of 1988.

All rights reserved; no part of this publication may be reproduced, stored in a retrieval system, or transmitted in any form or by any means, electronic, mechanical, photocopying, recording or otherwise without the prior written consent of the publisher or a licence permitting copying in the UK issued by the Copyright Licensing Agency Ltd, www.cla.co.uk

ISBN 978-1-78222-610-9

All scripture quotations are from the King James version unless otherwise stated.

Book design, layout and production management by Into Print
www.intoprint.net
+44 (0)1604 832149

Contents

RENEW YOUR MIND 4

PRAYER 22

ATTITUDE 36

PURPOSE 48

THE PROMISES OF GOD 52

ENCOURAGEMENT 53

ACKNOWLEDGEMENT 54

PRAYER OF SALVATION 59

RENEW YOUR MIND

Renew your mind means to see things in the eyes of God Almighty and not in your own mind. How you will renew your mind: by changing the way you think. How you will change the way you think: by meditating on the words of God.

Renew your mind will enable you to come out of your old way of doing things. Renew your mind will help you to transform your mind and help you to prove what is the good and acceptable perfect will of God. Your mind is a tool, your mind is a battlefield. Your mind is an important tool. You are the controller of your mind, for good or bad. Your mind can build you or destroy you.

I think I am in a better place to write about renewing your mind, because of what I have been through in the past years. Moreover, they say that experience is the best teacher and the lessons from experience are very powerful. I was in a situation in which my mind was under attack from the enemy. It was terrible that I nearly lost my mind; I never believed that such a thing could happen to me in the church. The shock I had when heard what they said about me - their lies, their set up, and blackmail - was unbelievable. That is why you have to be very careful about people you call your pastor, your mama and your papa. Blessed is the man that trusteth in the Lord and whose hope the Lord is. The same people can build up and can destroy you. We are in a wicked world. Jeremiah the prophet said: the heart is deceitful above all things and desperately wicked; who can know it?

It is when I started reading my Bible on my own and I got to a place where God said: forgive your enemies, pray for them; and I got to Romans 12 vs 2 which talks about *renewing your mind*. After reading these scriptures I started praying for the healing of my mind.

Our mind is who we are, therefore we must take care and guard it against the corrupting influences that are everywhere in our world. When a man engages his mind, he cannot be trapped in any situation. You have to shrewdly discern the subtle voices that are constantly presenting seemingly appealing ideologies, which are, in fact, opposed to God. You have to train yourselves, through the scriptures, to discern good from bad. We have to guard our hearts and minds through prayer and upright thoughts.

Paul gave us assurance that God will guard our hearts and minds when we surrender everything to Him in prayer. Moreover Paul let us know what we can think about in our mind: whatever that is good, pure, lovely, admirable, and worthy of praise. If anything is excellent or glorious, think about such things. It is very important and if you can think like that, you will have peace within yourself; because, as a man thinks in his heart, so he is!

A good thinker can overcome difficulties, including lack of resources, which often leave poor thinkers at the mercy of good thinkers. Your mind controls your future. Develop your mind with positive mental thinking. Powerful thinkers make powerful results. Quality thinking will bring you out of poverty. One man James Allen says: all that a man achieves or fails to achieve, is a direct result of his thoughts. Do you agree with him? If you accept it, you will place a high value on good thinking and make it a priority in your life. You know good thinkers look for the best, not the worst.

> [ISAIAH 26 VS 3] Thou wilt keep him in perfect peace whose mind is stayed on thee; because he trusteth in thee.

Moreover in life, whatever your mind accepts,

you will become; because your min
we live. When you allow what som
or does to upset you, you are allow
control you. It is very important to
people; what matters is what God said. ...
is another thing you have to understand: when
you know who you are, nobody can limit you or
hold you back. I'm a living testimony, and I am
in university now in my 60s. God said all things
work together for your good, to them that love
God.

> "You need the right people with you, not the best people."
>
> *Jack Ma*

Another way to renew our minds and to see our lives transformed is to go to the very root of the problems we are facing. Until we get to the issue we are not really renewing our minds at all. That is the fact because the choices you make today will determine your positions tomorrow. That is why you have to renew your mind because your mind is under attack every day. Our minds are a fascinating creation as this is the place where reality begins. Moreover the solution to every problem you face is contained in scripture. To be wise you must it. To be strong in faith you must believe it, to be successful in life you must practice it and faith is the secret of your success. Once you understand that, your struggle will begin to make sense.

When you renew your mind as God says your confidence and quietness shall be your strength. As you study God's word you will begin to experience the mind renewing and life-changing power he has deposited within you. Christ is able to do immeasurably more than all we ask or imagine according to his power that is at work with us. So start drawing on the power today. Do you know what's in you? There are words in the Bible that have so much life and power in them and are stronger than any therapy. God can give you a word that goes back into your past and heal your yesterday, secure your today, and anchor your tomorrow. That's why Satan clutters your life with so much junk that you don't have time for God's word. He knows it will unmask him and reveal the God potential that's lying dormant within you.

Before Jeremiah rose to prominence as a prophet God told him: *before I formed you in the womb I knew you*. Your parents didn't get the first look at you, God did. Nothing about you surprises him. In spite of what you have been through, he hasn't changed his mind about who you are or what you are destined to become before you were born. He set you apart. Stop looking for acceptance in the places where you don't belong. You are on a mission from God. That's why the enemy has tried so hard to take you out. Once you understand that, your struggles will begin to make sense. Only as you read God's word will you begin to understand the awesome mind-renewing, thirst-quenching, life-changing potential that was deposited within you from before the foundation of the world.

Any time you face opposition, know that you have a great position because Satan will never fight you if you have nothing to offer. Moreover don't let what won't matter tomorrow trouble your today. If you can take advantage of these words, the opinions of people will not determine where you will end up, but become irrelevant and don't count. I'm a living testimony because I never knew I would be a publisher. In the midst of my challenges I started discovering my potential and who I am, by renewing my mind in that difficult time. When you keep on renewing your mind, it will help you to discover that God's love is over your life. You are special, you are God's glory, and you are God's solution and it is working in you. God's wisdom is working over you. It doesn't matter what you are going through because you are blessed to be a blessing. A wise woman is the one that recognizes that life is not meant to be lived for self but that life was designed by the Creator to help other people, and to make a definite change in one's generation.

> "Don't judge someone's story by the chapter you walked in."

Praying women.com

[JEREMIAH 1 VS 5] **Before I formed thee in the belly I knew thee; and before thou camest forth out of the womb I sanctified thee, and I ordained thee a prophet unto nations.**

[PHILIPPIANS 4 VS 13] **I can do all things through Christ which strengthened me.**

When you renew your mind, all it takes is one daring decision. That's all it ever takes. When you move, God will move on your behalf, and if you don't move you will always wonder: what if? Our longest regrets are caused by our inaction. That is why we have to renew our mind and know what we want in our life. So, before you leave this earth, endeavour to give to others what God has entrusted in you. So many Christians never live their life; instead they are living other people's dreams. You see them going from one church to another, and at the end they never achieve anything in life. As you renew your mind-set, you will discover what God entrusted to you because it is inside you. When you doubt God you disappoint Him because He deserves better. So you must seek to strengthen your faith, because faith honours God and God honours faith. But with God on your side, you can say: whenever I'm afraid, I will trust in you. That will happen when you know who you are and renew your mind-set.

You see, the way you think determines the way you feel. And when your feelings become strong enough, that will determine the way you act. The person who says *cannot do it*, and the person who says *can do it*, are both right. Most of the time you set yourself up to be defeated by what you are saying. Your words reinforce either your right or wrong belief system.

Three times in First Peter, God reminds us to have a clear mind and self-control. Why? Because a clear mind is essential to self-control.

God gave us the power to choose our thoughts. Is that why Romans twelve verse two tells us to be transformed by working hard or by sheer willpower? No, what are we transformed by? The renewing of the mind. When your self-control is being tested, you need to fill your mind with the promises of God. Here's one: when you are tempted, he will also provide a way out so that you can stand up under the temptation. You must believe God when He says there's a way out for you. Paul writes: *I can do all things through Christ who strengthens me*. That means you can change and you can be different. Stop setting yourself up for failure by constantly criticising yourself. Don't allow *I'm no good* into your life. Nagging doesn't work on yourself or on anyone else. Instead say: *everything is possible for him who believes, and I believe*.

> [ROMANS 12 VS 2] and be not conformed to this world but be you transformed by the renewing of mind. That ye may prove what is that good and acceptable and perfect will of God.

Your mind is powerful enough to pick anything, because your mind is where you think good or bad. You have to control your mind by not using negative words. Your mind is more than mere imaginations; your mind is a mental picture with constructions or destructive capabilities. With your mind you can create things. Do you know that the mental construction of your mind is based on your imagination? It has the power to keep you in bondage or to liberate you, to be a better person. That is why you have to protect your mind by renewing it day by day.

You have to guard your heart and mind seriously because there are lots of TV programmes, movies, music and magazines that you won't watch if you want to be saturated and empowered by the Holy Spirit. You can guard your hearts and minds through the knowledge of God's word. We should not feed our minds with words that promote sinful thoughts. As a matter of fact, God cannot stop your thinking, be it good or bad; that is why you have to think positively to gain positive results. God, never says: let us pray together; instead He says: come let us reason together. That means your mind is needed, iron sharpening iron. In other words you are to pursue hard after God and put aside sinful thoughts with godly pursuits and mind-sets.

That's the principle of replacement. If you're

tempted to hate somebody, you replace those hateful thoughts with godly actions. Learn to be good to them, speak well of them and pray for them, and the peace of God, which passeth all understanding, shall keep your hearts and minds through Christ Jesus. Learn to pray, because prayer is the key; but working hard too is the key. Hard work will take you places in life. It will raise you to stand before kings and great people. Promotion comes with hard work. It is impossible to be diligent and work hard and remain poor. Success will come to the woman who works hard for it. Can I be honest with you? Any life that is not spent doing what it was created to do is a waste of time on earth. Apostle Paul said: *be careful for nothing; but in everything by prayer and supplication with thanksgiving let your requests be made known unto God.*

Renewing your mind is an important part of living a successful life. There are few principles that will help you better understand the concept of *renew your mind*. First, understand that God is not willing that any should perish. Not only is it His will for you to be saved but it is also His will for you to be free so you can know what is that good and acceptable and prefect will of God for your life. You need to know that

God reveals his will for mankind through his word. As you study and put God's word into practice you will come to understand God's will for your life.

That is why God said: *my thoughts are not your thoughts, neither are your ways my ways, saith the LORD. For as the heavens are higher than earth so are my ways higher than your ways, and my thoughts than your thoughts.*
[ISAIAH 55 VS 8]

When you renew your mind, there is no obstacle too hard for you; and when you stay focussed, you will achieve your goal. If you renew your mind it will enable you to see any challenges as opportunities. And you will achieve the greatness that is in you.

> "There are no great men, only great challenges that ordinary men are forced to meet"

William F. Halsey

As a matter of fact there is power in a quiet mind, because our creative mind is activated during times of mental quietness. John Maxwell gave his final thoughts by saying: "If you are not doing something with your life, it doesn't matter how long it is. If you are doing something with your life, it doesn't matter how long it is. Life does not come of years lived."

[PHILIPPIANS 4 VS 6 to 7] And the peace of God, which passeth all understanding, shall keep your hearts and minds through Christ Jesus.

Let us pray for peace, Lord, Your word says: "Thou will keep him in perfect peace whose mind is stayed on thee, because he trusteth in thee". Your word says: "The Lord gives strength to his people; the Lord blesses his people with peace". Your word says, "Peace I leave with you; my peace I give you. Do not let your heart be troubled and do not be afraid". Your word says, "The peace of God, which transcends all understanding will guard your hearts and your mind in Christ Jesus"

Today I need this peace which transcends understanding to settle my nerves and calm my mind. Instead of thinking about my fears and worries, help me to focus on your goodness, your faithfulness, your healing power, your overflowing resources, and your forgiving heart. Take up residence within me and fill me with your peace. Show me what's robbing me of it. I really want to know, Father, so I can be specific in what I need to confess, what I need to commit to and what I need to change. I open myself to you now. Teach me the secret of lasting peace. I thank You now for whatever it will take to help me receive the peace You have so generously offered to me. Your word says, "Let the peace of Christ rule in your hearts."

Today I want to be ruled by your peace instead of your fears and worries. So, I give all my concerns to you, trusting You to work them out for my good and Your glory. And God shall wipe away all tears from their eyes; and there shall be no more death, neither shall there be any more pain; for the former things are passed away. May the Lord bless you with what you work for. Grant you with what you hope for. And most of all surprise you with what you have not asked for. In Jesus name I pray. Amen.

> "Never speak from the reality of your circumstances but speak from the reality of God's future perspective. Very important."

Vivian Rodgers

Renewing your mind requires faith when acting on the word of God. You act on it just as you would act on the word of any honest man. You apply it in order to change the way you think about your life, your work, your relationships with everybody. Try to develop analytical thinking. Analytical thinking means you are able to identify and define a problem, extract key information from data and develop workable solutions for the problem identified in order to test and verify the cause of the problem and develop solutions to resolve the problem identified. In other words, analytical thinking is the ability to scrutinize and break down facts and thoughts into their strengths and weaknesses.

God is a free thinker. For you to renew your mind, you must be a thinker. Thinking is very hard, which is why so many people find it difficult to think. The person using analytical thinking sees things very differently because he or she will ask questions and want to know the facts. The ability to think helps you to be reasonable, and it will help you to develop yourself and not to compromise. An analytical person is more tolerant. A thinking person always analyses things. A thinking person wants to know the truth and is not afraid to offend anybody. Analytical thinking is good for your health, and people that think are always very constructive. Analytical thinking helps your mind. Always train your mind by reading because it will help your brain work better. The more our soul is transformed in such a way, the more the Lord thinks, by showing love and care to others.

[1 CORINTHIANS 3 VS 16] **For who hath known the mind of the Lord, that he may instruct him? But we have the mind of Christ.**

CONFESSION

My Lord I thank you for letting me know that I have to protect my mind, by not speaking any negative words, by taking control of my mind and renewing it day by day. And if I renew my mind it will transform me from glory to glory. Amen.

Satan always attacks our mind, even when it's our Lord Jesus. Satan attacked him by telling him: *if thou be the son of God, command that these stones be made bread*. Devil took Him up into the holy city and setteth on a pinnacle of the temple and saith unto him: *if thou be the son of God, cast thy self down*. But Jesus answered and said unto him: *it is written, Thou shall not tempt the Lord thy God because his mind is renewed*. He knew who Satan was, a deceiver and a liar, seeking whom he will destroy and kill. Moreover nothing becomes a reality in the life of any man until his mind is able to accommodate it.

[MATTHEW 2 VS 3 TO 6] And when the tempters came to Him, and he said if thou be the son of God command that these stones be made bread, but He answered and said it is written, man shall not live by bread alone, but by every word that proceeded out of the mouth of God. Then the devil taketh Him up into the holy city and setteth him on a pinnacle of the temple. And saith unto him, if thou be the son of God , cast thy self down , for it is written, He shall give his angels charge concerning thee, and in their hands they shall bear thee up, lest at any time thou dash thy foot against a stone. Jesus said unto him it is written again, thou shall not tempt the Lord thy God.

That is why as Christians we have to renew our minds every day, by speaking the word of God in our spirit, knowing that our weapons of our warfare are not carnal but pulling down the strongholds. How will you do that? By renewing your mind because Satan is after your destiny. That is why he is attracting your mind. If you fall by his lies, you will start seeing defeat, fear and failure. You start imagining what is going to happen to you. The devil is a liar. That is why God said cast down and bring it into captivity into God's obedience. We are at war in this world. That is why God said that our weapons of our warfare are not carnal but mighty through God for the pulling down of strongholds. We know that God makes everything work out according to his plan. Does that mean Paul understood every detail of God's plan? O no, but when he didn't understand the plan, he trusted the planner! And that's where Paul's peace, joy and contentment came from. The same is applicable to you. The almighty God withholds no good thing from those who do what is perfect in his sight.

PRAYER

Most of the time we pray for a certain thing, believing that whoever has a plan for our life is good for us. But God who has a plan for your life knows what would be good and what wouldn't be. Every negative memory that you refuse to nurture from yesterday will never have the strength to survive in your tomorrow. A woman of God Ruth - Billy Graham's wife – said that if God had answered all her prayers when she was young, she could have married the wrong man. And letting the peace of God rule in your hearts is very important. When God's peace rules your heart, you will never fall a victim.

A motivational speaker by the name of Zig Ziglar said: *what you picture in your mind, your mind will go to work to accomplish*. When you change your pictures, you automatically change your performance. Glory be to God. Obviously you know that each person is the principal factor that determines success in their life - that is way you have to think right, and stop thinking problems and stop thinking impossibilities. You must watch what goes into your mind, just be aware of what you think. Because as a person thinks in their heart, so is he or she. You know

God cannot do anything without our mind so your life can be limited by your thinking. People that are intelligent are the thinkers and their future is great because they are focussed and they read a lot.

> "Take risks, if you win you will be happy and if you lose you will be wiser."
>
> *Jason Statham*

[COLOSSIANS 3 VS 15] and let the peace of God rule in your hearts, which also ye are called in one body, and ye thankful.

[2 CORITHIANS 10 VS 4 TO 5] For the weapons of our warfare are not carnal but might through God to the pulling down of strongholds, casting down imaginations and every high thing that exalted itself against the knowledge of God and bring into captivity every thought to the obedience, of Christ.

CONFESSION

O God, help me to understand you ways and not to walk in my own integrity. Help me to trust in the Lord with all my heart and not to lean on my own understanding. That in all my ways I will acknowledge you and you will direct my paths. [Amen]

As believers we must go through life with consciousness of our spiritual position at all times. Often we may get into battles with our enemies because we lose sight of our heavenly position and the enemy pulls us down to his level. You mustn't get into flesh or allow yourselves to fall into his traps. It will become harder to fight him. But with consistent awareness of our spiritual authority, eventually you will override the enemy's attacks and subdue him. That is why you have to know the word of God for yourself. It will help you not be a victim and it will help you to stay focussed, not going from church to church.

If you can only learn how to close the door in your house and pray, the almighty will hear you because He never changes; He is a faithful God who said: *call up on me in the time of troubles. I will answer you, show you the things you knew not*. God cannot lie. His words are yes and amen. Hallulejah. He never says: *call upon pastor or bishop*; He says: *call on me*. The almighty God who never fails and He is not a respecter of anybody and He is not a God of partiality. If he can answer Esther the queen and her family, He will answer you. Just trust God and his words.

> "Don't be embarrassed by your failures, learn from them and start again."

Richard Branson

[EPHESIANS 6 VS 12] for we wrestle not against flesh and blood but against principalities, against powers, against the rulers of the darkness of this world and against spiritual wickedness in high places.

CONFESSION

Lord I thank you for giving me the ability to speak words of life and words that carry the power to alter my condition and destiny for good. I am so grateful to know that you delight in me and I become your pleasure. [Amen]

As Christians we have to guard our hearts because Satan will come to tell us that God's promise is not true. Most of the time he will make you feel bad about yourself. If you don't renew your mind, Satan will make you doubt God. That is why you have to read your Bible always. Look at Adam and Eve, how Satan made them question God's promise, even disobey

God's instruction. By asking Eve if it was true that God told her: *if you eat fruit of this tree in the garden, you shall surely die*? That is why you have to guard your heart because Satan is going like a lion but he is a dog seeking who he will deceive. He is a liar and a thief. You see, the flow of the mind and thinking determines the flow of the miraculous.

> [GENESIS 3 VS 1 TO 2] Now the serpent was more subtle than any beast of the field which the Lord God had made. And he said unto woman, yea hath God said ye shall not eat of every tree of the garden? And the woman said unto the serpent, we may eat of the fruit of the tree of the garden; but of the fruit of the tree which is in the midst of the garden, God hath said, ye shall not eat of it, neither shall ye touch it, lest ye die.

That is why you have to renew your mind by using the word of God and meditate on his promises. When you allow the word to transform your mind it will take you in a high level. That is when we can obtain the clam, undisturbed mind that the scripture describes. It is a mind that is not moved by circumstances, negative situations or the scare tactics of

Satan. When your mind-set is renewed, it will enable you to be Christ-like, not being afraid of anything at any time. And you will not listen to the voice of your enemy. Many people begin to doubt God for the supply of their needs or for healing, when Satan gets them to question the infelicity of God's covenant words. God cannot lie; whatever He says comes to pass because He is God, not man. Put your trust in God; He never fails you.

Your mind is more important than your body. You have to develop your mind so that you can pick the right thing, because your mind is a battlefield. Some of us think so little of ourselves that we'd rather be in a bad relationship than none at all. Being around people doesn't guarantee you won't feel lonely. Actually, being with the wrong people guarantees you will end up feeling empty and used. Until you overcome your fear of being alone and wait for God to give you the right relationships, you will continue to feel lonely. Sometimes loneliness is more about not liking yourself than about not having people around who like you. Otherwise, why would you spend so much energy avoiding rejection instead of building healthy relationships? Perhaps you think if you don't get involved you won't get hurt. Or you are afraid to open up in case people criticise you for sharing anything personal. Such anxieties just contribute to your sense of isolation. That is why you have to renew your mind day by day. Because the devil is after your destiny. David said: *you put me together inside my mother's body and I praise you because of the wonderful way you created me.* Everything you do is marvellous. Having these two pictures clearly in mind will stop you from operating with a devalued self-image and enable you to ask for what you need in a relationship.

> "Don't let the noise of other people's opinion drown out your own inner voice."
>
> *Steve Jobs.*

[PSALMS 139 VS 13 TO 14] **For thou hast possessed my reins; thou hast covered me in my mother's womb. I will praise thee; for I am fearfully and wonderfully made; marvellous are thy works well; and that my soul knoweth right well.**

[PHILIPPIANS 4 VS 19] **But my God shall supply all your need according to his riches in glory by Christ Jesus.**

[EPHESIANS 1 VS 18] The eyes of your understanding being enlightened; that ye may know what is the hope of his calling and the riches of the glory of his in heritance in the saints.

CONFESSION

The word of God dwelling in you richly. With all wisdom and spiritual understanding. Our life today is the expression and manifestation of God's word. I live a transcendent life today. Above poverty, sickness, disease; in Jesus name. Amen

When we receive Jesus, we receive eternal life and our spirits are instantly recreated in eternal life. Our spirit is instantly recreated and transformed from a dead spirit that was disconnected from God to a spirit that is reconnected to life of God. This is the first step when you renew your mind. The abundant grace inside us gives us power to renew our mind. That is why in the Bible it says that *therefore if any man be in Christ, he is a new creature, old things are passed away be hold all things are become new.*

When we renew our mind it helps us to possess power in his word and it enables us to walk in a level of dominion that supersedes anything in this world. When the spirit of God is resident in our spirit by renewing our mind, it gives us the edge as a Christian and helps us not to be subject to ungodly desires. That is why you have to yield yourself to the word of God. God speaks to you through his word, he tells you what to do through his word. He is the one who helps you to progress.

Once we renew our mind by seeing things the way God programmed for us, our life will be transformed from glory to glory. God said that Holy Spirit will teach us all things and show us how to handle our problems. Obviously when you allow the spirit of God to take you over, it will help you to develop the fruit of spirit, which is love, joy, peace longsuffering, gentleness, goodness, faith, meekness and temperance. Obviously in order to change your life, you must first change your thinking. And that's not easy when you have spent your life thinking a certain way.

Dr Frank Crane said our best friends and our worst enemies are our thoughts. To change your thinking, you must do it one thought at a time. That calls for discipline and determination. But it's worth it. If you wanted to compete in a marathon you wouldn't go on an all-sugar diet, would you? The fuel you put into something determines its performance. Yet we disregard this basic piece of wisdom; what you feed everything else is nothing compared to what you feed your mind. The good news is that if you want to transform 'you', think excellent thoughts! What enters your mind repeatedly, occupies it, shapes it, controls it and in the end expresses itself in what you do and who you become. Your mind will absorb and reflect whatever it's exposed to. The events you attend, the relationships you build, the materials you read or don't read and the thoughts you entertain all shape your mind, and eventually your character and your destiny. Start each day by praying; Lord, I want the kind of mind your word describes. One that's filled with excellent and honourable thoughts. Can you imagine what your life would be like if you constantly prayed that way and programmed your thinking accordingly? As a matter fact, you need to renew your mind-set, that's a place you will discover the real you.

> [GALATIANS 5 VS 22] **But the fruit of the spirit is love, joy, peace, longsuffering, gentleness, goodness, faith.**

[ROMAN 6 VS 13] **Neither yield ye your members as instrument of unrighteousness unto sin; but yield yourselves unto God, as those that are alive from the dead and your members as instruments of righteousness unto God.**

JOHN 14 VS 26] But the comforter, which is the Holy Ghost whom the Father will send in my name, He shall teach you all things and bring all things to your remembrance. What so ever I have said unto you.

CONFESSION

We rejoice because God has given us eternal life and granted us the power of attorney to live in and by the name of Jesus. We celebrate the life of peace, glory, progress, prosperity, success and victory He brought us into, in Jesus name. Amen.

When you focus your mind on God's promise, it will enable you to see yourself as God sees you. As you trust God and keep his commandments, it will transform you into success and good health. Spend time in the word of God and you will never have a negative mind-set. With your new mind-set you can never think failure, weakness, bitterness or being angry about anybody. That is why you should guard your heart with all diligence, for out of it are issues of life. The solution to every problem you face is contained in scripture. To be wise you must study by reading books and your Bible. To be successful in life, you must practice it. To be strong in faith you must believe it. Once you understand that, your struggle will begin to make sense. As you study God's word, you will experience the mind-renewing, life-changing power he has deposited with you. Know him who is able to do immeasurably more than all we ask or imagine according to his power that is at work with us. So start drawing on the power today.

> [PHILIPPIANS 4 VS 13] I can do all things through Christ which strengthened us.

You must continually acknowledge that your strength isn't your physical abilities but your Lord, for without Him you can do nothing. Learn the value of meditation on the word of God. The word has the ability to create and produce opportunities and guidance for you. The word enlarges your vision. Refuse to see lack and want. Look beyond the horizon and let the word propel you to prosperity. If you build your faith strong in God's word, you will neither cry nor cast down. Your faith grows when you hear God speak and it works when you do what He says. Always ask God's wisdom and never share your testimony to people you don't know, because the devil goes to church. As a matter of fact when you live your life this way, it will enable you not to live a begging life. In life sometimes God puts us in a difficult place to show his glory. Sometimes people see trouble or challenges and panic and they lose their focus, but they don't realise that in troubles and challenges is opportunity for a new level. Don't let your fear be your reality. Always be positive in life because you only live once; it's only JAMES BOND who LIVE TWICE! God has perfect timing, never early, never late; it takes a little patience and it takes a lot of faith. But it is worth the wait.

> "Grow up but don't give up."

Katy Perry

[PROVERBS 4 VS 23] **Keep thy heart with all diligence, for out of it are issues of life.**

[PROVERBS 12 VS 14] **A man shall be satisfied with good by the fruit of his mouth and the recompense of man's hands shall be rendered unto him.**

CONFESSION

God can bring peace to your past, purpose to your present and hope to your future.

[PROVERB 4 VS 12] **When thou goest thy steps shall not be straitened and when thou runnest, thou not stumble.**

CONFESSION

I am the child of most high, I can never be defeated. I can do all things through Christ which strengthened me. The highest God said I am a chosen generation and a royal priesthood. A city that can never be moved. Hallelujah.

ATTITUDE

As you gain knowledge of God's word, it will transform you in to the Godly kind of life. As you continue with the word of God you will discover who you really are. You will be transformed into all the word says about you. It said that you are beautiful, marvellously and excellently crafted, a victor and conqueror. This is God's perception of you and it's the image you must allow to dwell in your subconscious. That is why you have to develop the right attitude by renewing you mind. It will enable you to develop happiness, which is a fruit of the spirit. If you have the right attitude, you will maintain a fearless life in the midst of trouble because the word of God is life.

Your attitude is a powerful tool for positive action. Attitude is everything you do. The way you handle matters and the way you handle opposition. As a matter of fact, you don't need to buy it, but you have to develop it. In other words, to have a good attitude, you must accept responsibility for what goes inside your mind by monitoring your internal dialogue. When you renew your mind, you will never feel discouraged from any source because it is not God sending it your way. Immediately reject it and if you have no other source of encouragement, then do what David did. The Bible says that he encouraged himself in the Lord. When you feel yourself starting to lose courage, talk to yourself. Tell yourself you have made it through difficulties in the past and you will make it again. Remind yourself of past victories, make a list of your blessings and read them out loud any time you feel you are starting to sink emotionally.

As a matter of fact we're so busy trying to avoid personal pain, fear, and anger instead of trying to help others. Perhaps we should for once in our lives put ourselves in God's capable hands, telling Him how we feel and what happened to us. That will help us develop confidence in ourselves. So many times our outward appearance shows the way we are feeling inside. But it can also work the other way. When we look confident on the outside, we can feel more confident on the inside. Don't slump your shoulders and hang your head down. You are full of God life. So act like it, live with passion, zeal and enthusiasm. Don't just try to make it through the day but celebrate the day and say this is the day the Lord has made, I will rejoice and be glad in it. Don't dread the day but attack the day. Know what you want and accomplish it today and go for it. In life you will meet two types of people, one will build you up and the other will tear you down. In the end you will thank them both. Very important.

> [PSALMS 118 VS 24] This is the day which the Lord hath made; we will rejoice and be glad in it.

Don't live constantly comparing yourself with others. By renewing your mind you will be enabled to celebrate who God has made you to be. There is only one who has the unique traits and skills that make up who you are. God knew what He was doing and so rely on the thought that surely God said the something about you as He did when He called the world in to creation. And it was good. Have faith in God so that you never have regrets about yesterday because the regrets of yesterday and of tomorrow are enemies of today's happiness. God doesn't live in your yesterday and He doesn't triumph in your fears. All He expects of you is to love who God has made you and enjoy the simple little things of life that God has given to you. You really can't enjoy spiritual realities. So first start out by appreciating yourself and then also people God has placed in your world. You can also learn to let go of your past experiences, especially the unpleasant ones, and have no fret or fear of tomorrow.

> [PSALMS 37 VS 24 TO 25] though he fall, he shall not be utterly cast down; for the Lord upholdeth him with his hand. I have been young and now am old; yet have I not seen the righteous forsaken nor his seed begging bread.

That is why you don't talk about yourself according to the way you feel or look. Speak God's word over your life. Don't say about yourself what others say unless what they are saying is worth repeating. Maybe people decide to undo you with lies and blackmail. They may not have known any better, but the good news is you don't have to be affected by their words for the rest of your life. You can change your image of yourself; beginning right now, enjoy yourself because you are God special, and you are the light of the world. You are too loaded to be molested. Never have you lost confidence because of their talk. Don't give them attention. Always put your trust in God and his word. The word of God is in the womb of your miracle. So speak the word of God; it's never failed and it is life to a dying body.

Obviously when you renew your mind and

discover your purpose, nobody is big enough to stop you. Because you always have enough to create what you need. You may not recognise it yet, but it's there just waiting to be tapped. Stop saying I don't have what it takes; God's given you everything you need, and to get you where you ought to be. Start looking in the mirror! Go ahead, hug yourself and announce yourself: *I am full of untapped potential*. Until you pull out what God's placed within you, you will be like a spectator envying the success of others. Never allow the voice of fear to silence your internal voice. God has placed a compass in your spirit and if you follow the compass needle, it will lead you to your wealth place. God will use different people at different times to meet different needs in your life. He used Pharaoh to feed the Israelites. Imagine that, when famine hit, He led His people down to Egypt and made Pharaoh feed them for 400 years. Get this; when you ask God for something, don't dictate to Him who He will use to meet your need; God can even use your enemy to bless you. So chill out and enjoy the journey of life.

> [ROMANS 8 VS 35] who shall separate us from the love of Christ? Tribulation, Blackmail, Distress, or Persecution of Famine or Nakedness or Peril or Sword. As it is

written, for thy sake we are killed all the day long; we are accounted as sheep for the slaughter. Nay, in all these things we are more than conquerors through him that loves us.

CONFESSION

We live in victory, success, health, joy in the Holy Ghost and righteousness because that's the life God has ordained for us. We are seed of Abraham, through us the world is blessed. We are the salt of the earth and by our words we are preserved. In Jesus name.

> [ROMAN 8 VS 9] But ye are not in the flesh, but in the spirit, if so be that the spirit of God dwell in you. Now if any man have not the spirit of Christ, he is none of his.

Be acquainted with the words of God by study and meditate on them. Remember that the word of God will bring you to the same conclusion as Moses. You will see that the word is your life, which is why Moses knew the ways of God while the children of Israel were only acquainted with the acts of God. But they saw God's words as commandments to obey. But to Moses it was life. Do you know that the word of God is the mirror of God that reflects your spiritual image and it reveals God's opinion and perception of you? There is glory and fulfilment that you will experience in your life as soon as your spirit gets hold of the picture of you. You have to realize that God's word was given to you to reflect God picture of you; it will change your perspective on your life.

CONFESSION

I affirm that the spirit of God has granted me everything I require to live triumphantly on earth. I am excellent, sound, fruitful and productive in every good work. Christ is glorified in me forever, and his righteousness is unveiled through me. I am the workmanship of God, created in Christ Jesus for his works. I have God's righteousness, life and nature. I am the effulgence of his glory and the express image of his person. Therefore I think, act and live as his perfect representation here on the earth.

> [2 CORITHIANS 3 VS 18] **But we all with open face beholding as in a glass the glory of the Lord are changed into the same image from glory to glory. Even as the spirit of the Lord.**

> [2 CORINTHIANS 2 VS 14] **Now thanks be unto God which always causeth us triumph in**

Christ and maketh manifest the savour of his knowledge by us in every place.

[ROMANS 8 VS 15 TO 16] **For ye have not received the spirit of bondage again to fear, but ye have received the spirit of adoption whereby we cry Abba father. The spirit itself breath witness with our spirit that we are the children of God.**

When you are now living by the spirit of God, it will help you to be stay able in all your doing because Christ in you is the hope of your glory. When you have the right mind in Christ it will quicken your mortal bodies. The word of God has power when you know how to use it, by opening your mouth and meditating on the word of God and testifying his goodness in your life. Because God cannot lie. God is not a respecter of anybody; if he can do it for others, he will do it for you.

[ROMANS 8 VS 11] **But if the spirit of him that raised Jesus up from the dead dwell in you, he that raised up Christ from the dead shall also quicken your mortal bodies by his spirit that dwell in you.**

[ECCLESIASTS 8 VS 4] **Where the word of a king is, there is power.**

[1 CORINTHIANS 2 VS 12] **Now we have received not the spirit of the world but the spirit which is of God; that we might know the things that are freely given to us of God.**

CONFESSION

We know that all things are working together for our good, and wherever we go the favour of God is going with us. We know that nothing can separate us from God because we are blessed in going out and blessed in coming in. God with us will overcome every trouble we face.

When you get acquainted with the word of God, it will help you to take responsibility for yourself. You have to know that Christianity is for talkers. The word of God in your mouth is your assurance for a glorious, prosperous and successful future. That is why Jeremiah said that the word of God is like a fire and like a hammer that breaketh the rock in pieces. Christianity is not religion, but relationship. Christianity is everyday work by speaking the word in faith, by renewing your mind because your mind is a battlefield. That is why Satan is after your mind to destroy you.

[JEREMIAH 23 VS 29] **Is not my word as a fire?**

Saith the Lord and like a hammer. That breaketh the rock in pieces.

Jeremiah said he found the words of God and ate them, because the word of God is life, when you find it. That is why you have to study your Bible to help you in time of trouble. The word of God being God's light, which describes or defines your true identity and personality. When you study or learn God's word, you will discover more about yourself. It will help you to locate yourself in Him. As you develop the love from the word of God, you will transform to be a better person and you will make positive changes. Do you know that the word of God is a lamp unto your feet and a light on your path? It will help develop confidence in yourself.

> [JEREMIAH 15 VS 16] Thy words were found and did eat them. And thy word was unto me the joy and rejoicing of mine heart for I am called by thy name. O Lord God of hosts.

CONFESSION

The word of God is alive in me; I'm making progress and profiting on every side. I am healthy, strong, excellent and vibrant. My heart is a fertile ground and the word of God is producing great results in every area of my life. I am one with the father; as Jesus is so am I in this world. Glory be to God.

> [PSALM 119 VS 105] **Thy word is a lamp unto my feet and a light unto my path.**
>
> [PSALM 119 VS 89] **For ever, O Lord thy word is settled in heaven.**
>
> [PSALM 119 VS 130] **The entrance of thy words giveth light it giveth understanding unto the simple.**

CONFESSION

Our lives have been given a meaning. Therefore we are impacting the lives of those around us positively. We are living meaningful lives. Thanks be to God. We rejoice because it's given unto us to understand your word and hear your voice in our spirit. Thankyou for the influence of your word in our life. In Jesus name.

Renew your mind means your mind-set has to change because many people are stagnant with the wrong mind-set. That leads them to question God or doubt God's promise. Because of this wrong mind-set, they become a victim by going from one church to another. They never enjoy God's benefit because the word of

God is not true in their life. When you keep the word in your heart and in your mouth day and night, it will produce a new mind-set of victory, success and advantage. Make sure you keep pondering, muttering and shouting the word.

For you to have a good mind-set, you have to a place what is conducive where you can shout your mind down and talk your spirit up with the word. Make sure you practise and you will have a renewed mind-set. You will notice that you talk differently and your friends notice that there is something unique about you; most of them will not like you because they feel that you have become full of yourself. Don't take any notice of them, because we are running heaven's race. That is why you keep the word in your mouth and you will come back with a testimony. Meditate on the word of God to help build you up and enable you to develop spiritual and mental attitudes that are consistent with God's will and purpose for your life.

PURPOSE

When you renew your mind, it will help you to discover your purpose. What is purpose? Purpose is the master of motivation and mother of commitment. Purpose is the source of enthusiasm and womb of perseverance. Purpose is the key of life. Moreover life without purpose has no meaning. Do you know that your vision is buried in your purpose? You have to understand that without knowledge of purpose, life becomes an endless string of activities with little or no significance. You are created with purpose. This is the reason you are born. Bill Gates is an example of someone who discovered his purpose early by thinking about software. Bill Gate's story shows you how much you can achieve when you discover your purpose early. Bill Gates didn't waste his time pursuing another thing and he didn't even complete his degree at Harvard University. That is why Myles Munroe said that "When the purpose of a thing is not known, abuse is inevitable."

The greatest tragedy in a human life is not death, but life without purpose. Purpose is the key to life, without purpose life has no meaning. That is why so many people are living a life of regret. When people live a life without purpose, they start saying "I'm surviving" because they miss their purpose in life. However if you develop your purpose, it will help you to be yourself and enable you to do the right thing. Very important: if you don't discover your purpose, Satan will find you one!

Great minds have purpose, other have wishes. A life without a purpose cannot have a definite plan. Moreover if you continue doing the wrong things you will never be able to create time to discover your purpose nor start working at it. When you make a decision to live for your purpose, you will never regret it. Every human being is born with purpose in this world, and God created them with gifts and talents and God expects us to develop them. Moreover we use these talents to better our self and others. The most important thing you need to do to accomplish your purpose is to stop, get comfortable, sit down and find time for thinking.

CONFESSION

I make the right choice in my life because Jesus in me is greater than wrong desires in me. I will live and not die. God's strength in me trumps my weakness. Despite my flaws, my destiny is being fulfilled!

[EPHESIANS 1 VS 3] Blessed be the God and the Father of our Lord Jesus who hath blessed us with spiritual blessing in heavenly places in Christ.

[1 THESSALONIANS 2 VS 13] For this cause also thank we God without ceasing, because, when ye received the word of God which ye heard of us, ye received it not as the word of men, but as it is the truth, the word of God, which effectually worketh also in you that believe.

CONFESSION

As we wait on God, whosoever comes against us shall fall. As we wait on God, know evil will be in our place. As we are planted in the house of God, we will eat the best in the land. Wherever they are calling us for evil, let the God of vengeance answer them by thundery. In Jesus name.

Renew your mind by meditating on God's word and applying it; that is why God has given us His word as a lamp to our feet and a light to our path to lead us to Him. Thy words have I hid in my heart that I might not sin against thee. With the words of God in our mouths, we will not back slide.

Lord, cultivate in me an appetite for your word. Thank you that the Bible is food for my soul. Lead me to read it, to savour it, to ingest it and to know the strength that your words can give to my often failing heart.

THE PROMISES OF GOD

[ISAIAH 3 VS 10] Say ye to the righteous, that it shall be well with him; for they shall eat the fruit of their doings. [Amen]

[EZEKIEL 36 VS 9 TO 11] For behold I am for you, and I will turn unto you, and ye shall be tilled and sown; And I will multiply upon you man and beast; and they shall increase and bring fruit and I will settle you after your old estates, and will do better unto you than at your beginnings and ye shall know that I am the Lord's. [AMEN]

[PSALMS 62 VS 5 to 8] My soul, wait thou only upon God; for my expectation is from him. He only is my rock and my salvation; he is my defence; I shall not be moved, I Trust in him at all times; ye people, pour out your heart before him; God is a refuge for us. Selah. [AMEN]

[PSALMS 82 VS 6] I have said, Ye are gods; and all of you are children of most High. [AMEN]

[PSALMS 34 VS 5] They looked unto him; and were lightened; and their faces were not ashamed. [AMEN]

ACKNOWLEDGEMENT

I have written others books COMING TO LONDON, BE YOURSELF AND DON'T GIVE UP YOUR HOPE IN GOD. Glory be to God. I just use this opportunity to thank God for My Big mama, my pastor, my mentors and my role model who went to be with the Lord this year. May she rest in peace. She is a woman of integrity, a praying woman. Miss you. Always there to pray for me. Big mama I miss you, you know how I love you. But God knows the best. Rest in peace. Nobody born of a woman can take your place in my life.

Thank God for my children, always there to assist me. Always there praying for me. Theo Daniels played the most important part in making the book succesful.

And I thank God for Kemi Anigiobi for her assistance. God bless you all.

Lord we realise that focusing on our troubles causes us to forget that even in the midst of trials You are good. Teach us the art of a grateful heart. Thanksgiving is a virtue that grows through practice.

ENCOURAGEMENT

Love the Lord with all your mind and heart. Let God be your first priority. Never give up your dreams no matter what. Never be a quitter. Quitters never accomplish their assignment. Quitters never achieve their goals. Always inspire yourself. Never stay where they tolerate you, go where they celebrate you because you are a mirror of God and you are God righteousness. All it took was one daring decision; that's all it ever takes. When you move, God will move on your behalf. And if you don't move, you will always wonder *what if*? Our longest regrets are our inactions – regrets about the things we would have, could have or should have done but did not do. So, the word for you is trust God and his words.

The choices you make today will determine your positions tomorrow and the seeds you sow today determine your harvest tomorrow. You don't need anybody's approval because you are God-chosen and God-special. Glory be to God. Learn to enjoy yourself because life is too short. Never be a people pleaser, rather be a God pleaser. That will help you. But remember that what you make happen to others, God will make happen to you, be it good or bad. So be good to people because the people you meet down, one day you will meet them up. God is not a respecter of persons.

Never put your trust in man. Love yourself; nobody will love you for you. You are the architect of yourself. Don't let your fear become your reality. Never be worried about things you cannot change. Don't allow people's opinion to affect you because you are wonderful-made and God-special. Never allow people's opinion to devalue you because nobody is better than you. It's only God's opinion that matters. People are people, God is God himself.

People like you the way you are, but when you come up high then it can become a problem. Because not everybody will celebrate your new you. So be yourself. Remember this: *new level new devil*. Ha ha ha. To God be the glory. When they set out to bring me down with lies, I nearly lost my mind because I never knew that such things could happen to me in the church. In Proverbs 24 vs 10 you'll read that, *If thou faint in the day of adversity, thy strength is too small*. Apostle Paul said *it is good for me that I have been afflicted; that I might learn thy statutes*.

[PSALMS 119 VS 71]

You see, in life never apologise for who you are because your enemies see your potential before you realise who you are. Just know the word of God in your spirit because it is able to build you up and give you your inheritance.

> "The best way to treat obstacles is to use them as stepping stones. Laugh at them, tread on them, and let them lead you to something better."

Enid Blyton

> "Frame your future with the words that give you confidence that you are not alone. Haters are the people who will broadcast your failure and whisper your success."

Will Smith

> "A winner is a dreamer who never gives up."

Nelson Mandela

CONFESSION

I declare that I am anointed of God, and that anointed removes every burden and destroys every yoke of infirmity. It causes me to live in dominion over sickness, disease and death, in the name of Jesus Christ. [Amen]

Dear Lord, we are prone to look out for ourselves. Give us wisdom to know when giving up our rights would best demonstrate your love and grace to others. Our life helps paint our neighbour's picture of God.

Remember the poor, the needy, the stranger, the widow; when you help them, you are doing it for God. No one has seen God, but God sees us. Go to the motherless home and bless them too. Look inside your family - they need help, because charity begins at home. You should take care of your family and people close to you before you go about helping others. Because it is more blessed to give than to receive. Lord may we these days have eyes to see other's needs, and direction from you on any ways we might help, and the spirit to obey. May we live out the faith love and hope you have given to us. Amen.

New International Version. [Proverbs 19;17] says, *Whoever is kind to the poor lends to the Lord;*

and he will reward them for what they have done. God cannot lie.

> [MATTHEW 25 VS 38 TO 40] **When saw we thee a stranger, and took thee in? or naked, and clothed thee? Or when saw we thee sick, or in prison and came unto thee? And the King shall answer and say unto them, Verily I say unto you, In as much as ye done it unto one of least of these my brethren, ye have done it unto me.**

> [PSALMS 41 VS 1 to 2] **Blessed is he that considereth the poor; the Lord will deliver him in time of trouble. The Lord will preserve him, and keep him alive; and he shall be blessed upon the earth; and thou will not deliver him unto the will of his enemies.**

CONFESSION

I have God righteousness, life and nature. I am the effulgence of His glory and the express image of His person. Therefore I think, act and live as his perfect representation here on the earth.

PRAYER OF SALVATION

Will you accept Jesus as your Lord and Saviour today?

The Bible reads, *If thou shalt confess with thy mouth the Lord Jesus, and shall believe in thine heart Jesus hath raise from the dead, thou shalt be saved. For with the heart man believeth unto righteousness; and with the mouth confession is made unto salvation.*

[Romans 10 vs 9 to 10]

To receive Jesus Christ as Lord and Saviour of your life, please pray this prayer from your heart today!

Dear Jesus, I believe that you died for me and rose again on the third day. I confess I am a sinner. I need your love and forgiveness. Come into my life, forgive my sins and give me eternal life. I confess you as my Lord and Saviour. Thankyou for my salvation, your peace and joy. Amen.

If you have made that confession, congratulations, you are born again and your life will not remain the same anymore.

Heavenly Father, may our behaviour today cause others to ask us why we are different. We ask that we follow your Holy Spirit's leading as we explain to them the hope that is in us. Live so that others will want to know Jesus.

If you need more information:

E-mail: vdaniels58@hotmail.com

Telephone: 02072494302

OTHER BOOKS BY VIVIAN DANIELS

ISBN 978-1-78222-081-7

ISBN 978-1-78222-093-0

ISBN 978-1-78222-451-8

Lightning Source UK Ltd.
Milton Keynes UK
UKHW021511171118
332514UK00004B/84/P